A Letter For You

A Collection of Handwritten Letters for Survivors

Letters Collected by Cyd Igot

Edited by Kim Bruce
Book Cover done by Stella Fernandez

Photography done by Mariana C. Barros, Kim Bruce, Marcian Costa, Stella Fernandez, Mekrina Knoll, Kindra Tully, Michael Yuenger, Shai Zohav

Disclaimer

The A Letter for You Project provides the aletterforyou.org website as a service to the public.

The A Letter for You Project is not responsible for, and expressly disclaims all liability for, damages of any kind arising out of use, reference to, or reliance on any information contained within the site. While the information contained within the site is periodically updated, no guarantee is given that the information provided in this website is correct, complete, and up-to-date.

Although the A Letter for You Project may include links providing direct access to other Internet resources, including websites, the A Letter for You Project is not responsible for the accuracy or content of information contained in these sites.

Links from the A Letter for You Project to third-party sites do not constitute an endorsement by the A Letter for You Project of the parties or their products and services. The appearance on the website of advertisements and product or service information does not constitute an endorsement by the A Letter for You Project, and the A Letter for You Project has not investigated the claims made by any advertiser. Product information is based solely on material received from suppliers.

Furthermore, use of aletterforyou.org is with the understanding that all images submitted become the property of the A Letter for You Project. Images are then used at the sole discretion of the A Letter for You Project, and without prior consent from submitting parties.

ISBN: 9781711009216

Letters Collected by Cyd Igot
Edited by Kim Bruce
Book Cover by Stella Fernandez
Photography by Mariana C. Barros, Kim Bruce, Marcian Costa, Stella Fernandez, Mekrina Knoll, Kindra Tully, Michael Yuenger, Shai Zohav

An Introduction and a Request

I began collecting these letters because I felt helpless and hopeless in the face of school shootings, violence, rape, cancer, the rise in suicides, bullying, trauma big or small, losing our veterans daily, and just getting weepy watching the news. I didn't know the right thing to say to the people in pain who mattered to me so I began to collect words of encouragement and support from strangers and post them on aletterforyou.org for people to find the letters when they needed them. The project is purposely anonymous to protect the privacy of survivors. It asks nothing from survivors; it simply offers the good intentions, the vulnerability, and the hope of strangers and some fellow survivors as well. When we say survivors, it can mean anyone who has survived a traumatic event or endured the heart-breaking, seemingly impossible odds of just waking up and conquering the simplest task of getting out of bed. We all know someone who suffered something we wish they didn't.

I have been humbled and overwhelmed by the thousands of letters I have seen people kiss, cry, and pray over. I have hugged countless strangers and have poured all of their anonymous love into this book, which I pray changes your life with its magic the way it has changed my own. There are now thousands of letters, but we need thousands more for every type of survivor out there. We request you leave the letters anonymous.

Please send your letters to:
A Letter For You
P.O.B. 472
Garrett Park, MD 20896

Or email: letters@aletterforyou.org

Help spread the word online through Twitter, Instagram and Facebook as well as sharing this book with someone you know who may be having a hard time in life right now...

Dedications

I dedicate this book to the sweet miracle that is Sofia and her resilient Mama Angela! This book was inspired by Doug's vulnerability along with Mekrina's strength, wisdom and sisterhood. I am constantly in awe of Felipe's fighting spirit, Simona's consistent daily checking in since 2nd grade and Liz's elegant grit . These ingredients have me believe in the endurance of the human spirit to not only to survive but to thrive so beautifully, I am often moved to tears.

Lastly, this book is dedicated to my nieces and nephews, 11 and counting and my god children... I hope we leave this earth better than we found it my little loves. I cannot ask that of each of you if I do not put some good into this world myself.

We are all in this together. I love you with my whole heart. Each of you restores my faith and hope in humanity.

Table of Contents

For All Survivors

❧

He was tall, dark, handsome and brooding. I interrupted his day with a smile and an invitation to write a letter for the project. Though he rolled his eyes with obvious irritation, he took out a piece of paper and humored me by jotting down the name of the website. I was embarrassed when he left because I am a people pleaser and he was very clearly not pleased!

I ran into the handsome giant again and he engulfed me in the warmest bear hug. The man that couldn't get away from me fast enough almost crushed my lungs with his welcome. He admitted to reading letters everyday since he stormed off with the website address in his pocket. He mentioned that he was finally hugging people in his life again and finally going on dates and being open to the world in ways he hadn't been for years. I was dumbfounded. I am not speechless ever.

He said there was no support out there for traumatized men where they didn't feel layers of shame or feel exposed. He exposed to me my own biases. Initially I had an inaccurate blueprint of who this project was for and who it would benefit. I'm happy to be wrong and he helped course correct my assumptions. This project is for every single person out there.

He confessed that he never did write a letter and I hugged him because he never had to. I was just happy that the letters moved him and inspired him to plug back into a created life of his choosing.

Disclaimer
If this topic is triggering, please skip this section and go to page 30

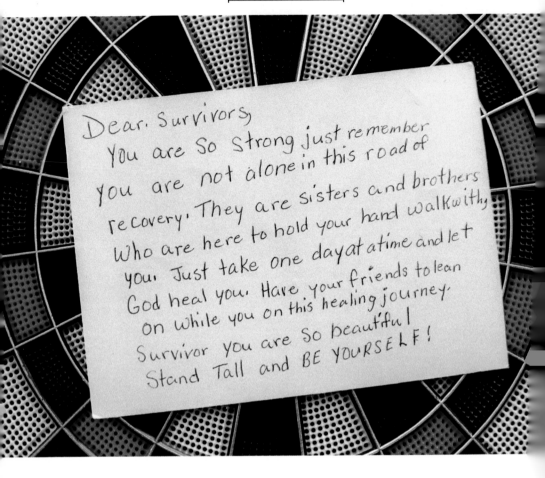

Dear Survivors,

You are so strong just remember you are not alone in this road of recovery.
They are sisters and brothers who are here to hold your hand walk with you. Just take one day at a time and let God heal you.
Have your friends to lean on while you on this healing journey.
Survivor you are so beautiful.
Stand Tall and BE YOURSELF!

Our lives take unusual turns when we least expect it and we
must understand we can and must find our way back to what
we think is normal. Find a true friend, let them share your load
as you lean on them. Be strong, be true to yourself and give in
sometime if you feel the need to be sad or cry. Be forgiving of
yourself always and give healing a chance to occur. Be all that
you can and normalcy will follow.

In peace.

You may survive by hanging on, but, you
might just thrive by letting go...

Time
Believe in that.
Survive.
Survival grants us time.
Survive!!!
Believe... Survive. Time. Believe.
Survive. Believe. Time.

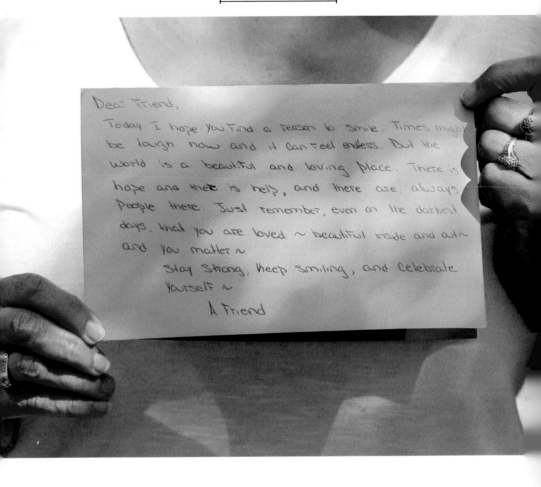

Dear Friend,

Today I hope you find a reason to smile. Time might be tough now and it can feel endless, but the world is a beautiful and loving place. There is hope and there is help, and there are always people there. Just remember, even on the darkest days, that you are loved ~ beautiful inside and out ~ and you matter ~

Stay strong, keep smiling, and celebrate yourself ~

A Friend

Please keep feeling
I know it hurts, but
YOU ARE NOT ALONE
Peace * rest * warmth * love

You are an inspiration

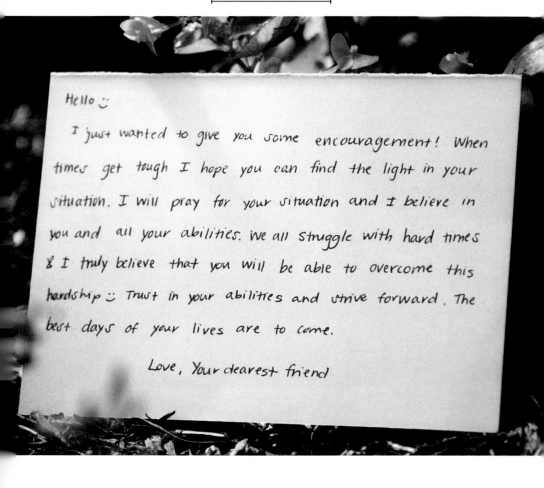

Hello =)

I just wanted to give you some encouragement! When times get
tough I hope you can find the light in your situation. I will pray
for your situation and I believe in you and all your abilities. We
all struggle with hard times and I truly believe that you will
be able to overcome this hardship =) Trust in your abilities and
strive forward. The best days of your lives are to come.

Love,
Your dearest friend

Dear friend,

Right now, you might not believe this, but it'll be more than okay, actually, it'll be GREAT. You're strong, you're resilient, YOU matter. If you don't believe that, just say it over and over and over until you do. You matter and I love you. Don't lose sight of how incredibly wonderful you are. Thank you for existing.

Love,
A friend

Dear Survivor,

You are worthy of experiencing intimacy. I used to believe I wasn't. You are. I love you.

Never forget that you matter
No matter what you're going through,
There is ALWAYS a bright light at the end of the tunnel.
Stay close to those that love you.
Don't be hesitant to ask for help.
There is always someone who cares.

Find a passion and follow it.

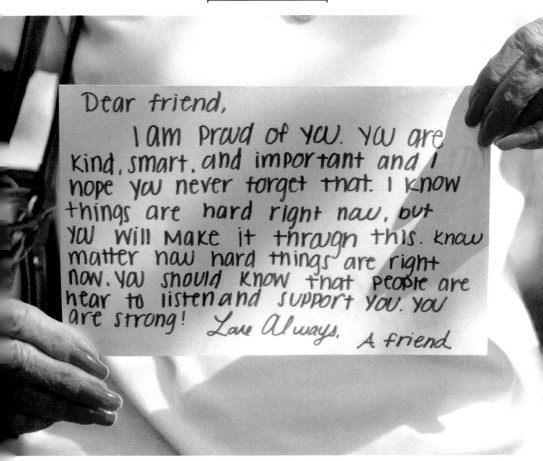

Dear friend,

I am proud of YOU. You are kind, smart and important and I hope you never forget that.. I know things are hard right now, but you will make it through this. No matter how hard things are right now, you should know that people are here to listen and support YOU. YOU are strong!

Love always,
A friend

I wonder how to help
people find the strength
they need and admire
those that do.

May you find the
strength to live +
love + stand up for all
that you deserve.

I wonder how to help people find the strength they need and admire those that do. May you find the strength to live and love and stand up for all that you deserve. <3

Believe you can and you're halfway there

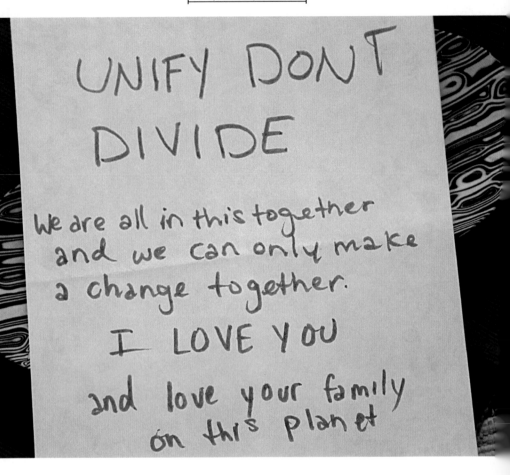

UNIFY DON'T DIVIDE
We are all in this together and we can only make a change together.

I LOVE YOU
And love your family on this planet.

What you are going thru now
It may not be fun but it's necessary and your strength, grace
and beauty will be revealed in time because this can only make
you a better version of you!

Please Repeat after me,

- I am Beautiful
- I am Confidant
- I am worthy
- I am lovable
- I am not perfect but I am Precious
- I have an amazing future and I am on my way!!
- My Dreams will come true
- I was created for a unique Purpose that will be fullfilled
- I am not defined by my circumstances, my past or my mistakes.
- I am forgiven of all my Sins
- I am healed
- I am blessed
- I am restored
- I am Joyful and full of Possibilities
- I can and will do this!!

* Jesus Loves ME!!

Now Repeat this "daily" until you Believe it !! :)

Love,
Refusing to give up.

P.S
  Be....
    Bold. Confidant. Determined (BCD)

Have A....
  Positive. Mental. Attitude. (PMA)
    Everyday!!

Dear friend,
   The weather is cold. If
I could I would give you
the biggest hug. Know that
in my heart I want to.
Know that you have a
beautiful spark inside
of you. The equality of
your human value is
undeniable.

Dearest survivor,

As hellish as life can truly be...
Keep dreaming... when you dream, hope, look up at the clouds and
stars, your spirit gets to exhale and you can't be defeated in
those moments! Head up!!

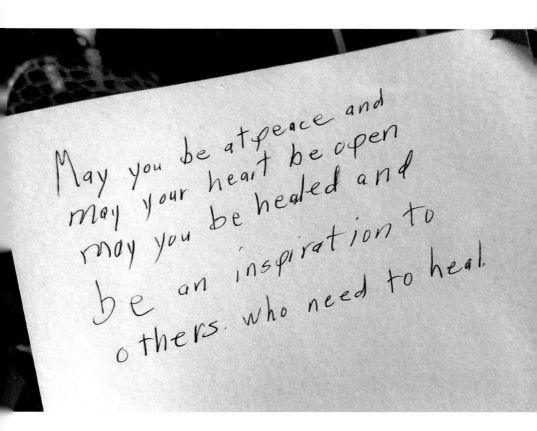

May you be at peace and may your heart be open..
May you be healed and be an inspiration to others who need to
heal.

10-22-14

The loneliness
we feel is
REAL & The
TRUTH is
we are NEVER
alone! Love
and understanding
is out there

ALWAYS REMEMBER TO SLAY

YOU ARE A ✴

YOU ARE THE CREAM OF THE CROP

OPULENCE

honey.

the world is yours

everything is yours

YOU ARE A QUEEN AND YOU
DESERVE EVERY HAPPINESS.

**Thinking
of You**

Put Your feet on the ground
without shoes on...
The ground is right there...
Sometimes that's the best
place to find yourself...
Sometimes that's All I have,
the ground...
You Choose... You going to RUN?
                             WALK?
                             STAY?
                             GO? STOMP?
                          or DANCE?

Put Your feet on the ground without shoes on...
The ground is right there...
Sometimes that's the best place to find yourself...
Sometimes that's all I have,
The ground...
You choose...
You going to RUN? WALK? STAY? GO? STOMP? Or DANCE?

Dear Survivor

We <3 you

Love,
The World
Happy Valentine's Day

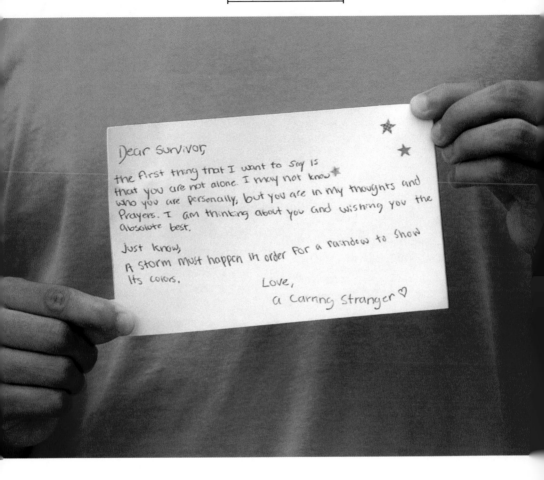

Dear Survivor,

The first thing that I want to say is that you are not alone. I
may not know who you are personally, but you are in my thoughts
and prayers. I am thinking about you and wishing you the
absolutely best.

Just know,
A storm must happen in order for a rainbow to show it's colors.

Love,
A caring stranger <3

Dear Stranger-

My whole heart aches at the idea that you feel alone in the world...

Love,
Someone who would just hold your hand!

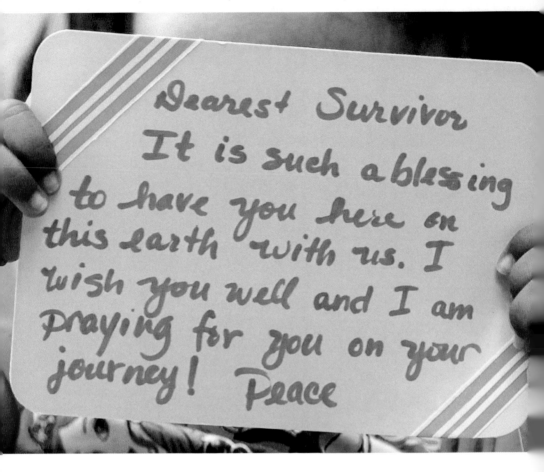

Dearest Survivor,

It is such a blessing to have you here on this earth with us.. I
wish you well and I m praying for you on your journey!

Peace

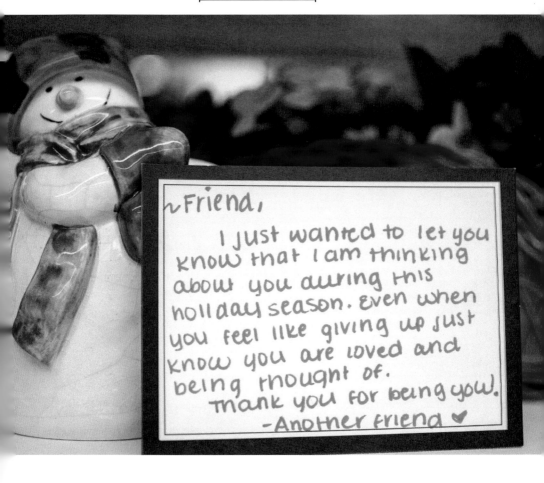

Friend,

I just wanted to let you know that I am thinking about you
during this holiday season.
Even when you feel like giving up just know you are loved and
being thought of. Thank you for being you!

-Another friend <3

Write a reflection, reaction, or letter...

_____

_____

_____

_____

_____

_____

_____

_____

_____

_____

_____

_____

_____

_____

_____

Feel free to send these reflections, reactions, or letters to
A Letter for You, P.O.B 472, Garrett Park, MD 20896

From Survivors

She wore what looked like her Sunday best, with a woven cardigan draped over her shoulders and a purse that looked as if it carried half her house and was half her own weight. She looked elegantly in her sixties and she kept walking around the A Letter For You Project display which typically has letters for people to read and blank cards for people to write on. I kept offering her a blank card but she looked irritated that I asked so often so, I gave her space. I kept awkwardly smiling at her because she was so curious about the table but kept a 3 foot radius for what seemed like 10 minutes. While I was helping someone else, I noticed her at the far corner of the table pulling out a dictionary. The revelation that what I interpreted as irritation was her getting the gumption up to contribute to someone else was beyond humbling. She did not slap together a letter but checked her spelling to honor those who would be reading it. My tender thought was that she was generous. She wrote a letter with an intentionality and determination that only revealed itself later in the evening.

The event I went to was meant for survivors of rape. There was a portion of the evening allotted for survivors to tell their stories. Imagine my surprise when this skittishly thoughtful lady, in her Sunday best, raised her hand. With a shaky but very strong voice, she recounted in details that left me weepy, that she had been violated late in life. She was gracious and did this brave thing to comfort and inspire others. When I consider her selflessness in writing a letter to another survivor, every piece of her had me in awe.

She wrote a letter and I never would have assumed she would have needed one herself. This project has had me realize survivors don't have a certain look and do not follow a template. Every single person has endured things I wish they did not. These letters are written for every single type of survivor and as an invitation to contribute to every kind of survivor regardless of what you are surviving yourself.

Disclaimer
If this topic is triggering, please skip this section and go to page 52

I just want to remind you that you're amazing! I am a lawyer and I work with survivors everyday and each survivor gives me so much hope and makes me grateful for you and everything I have in my life. Don't ever give up because you give me hope!

I just want to remind you that you're amazing! I am a lawyer and I work with survivors everyday and each survivor gives me so much hope and makes me grateful for you and everything I have in my life. Don't ever give up because you give me hope!

<3

It takes time
But your courage and persistence will create a path to healing.

I am a survivor...

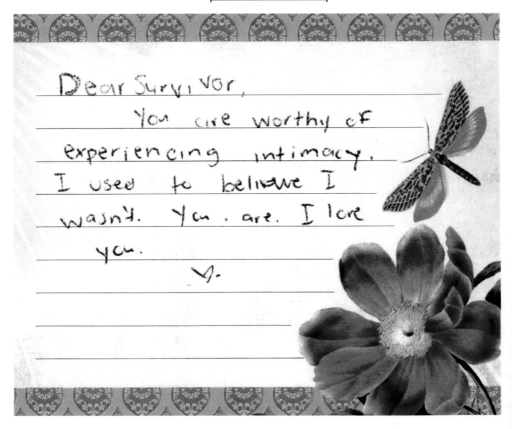

Dear Survivor,
You are worthy of experiencing intimacy. I used to believe I wasn't. You are. I love you.

-<3-

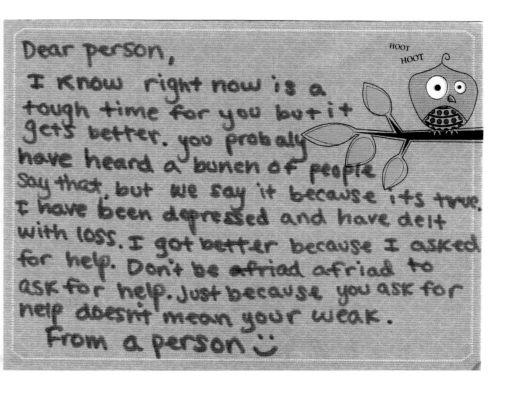

Dear Person,

I know right now is a tough time for you but it gets better. You probably have heard a bunch of people say that, but we say it because it's true. I have been depressed and have dealt with loss. I got better because I asked for help. Just because you ask for help doesn't mean you're weak.

From a person =)

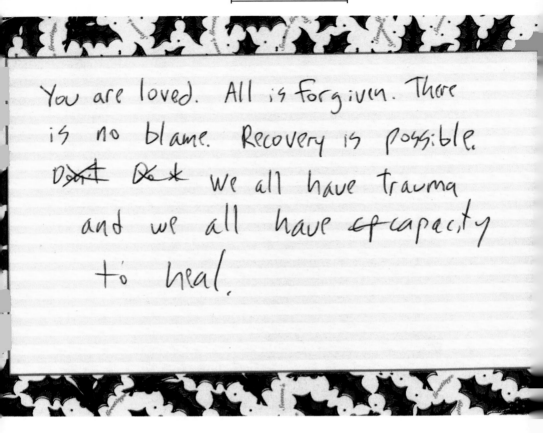

You are loved. All is forgiven. There is no blame. Recovery is possible. We all have trauma and we all have the capacity to heal.

Dear You,
You are wonderful. You are inspiring! YOU are AWESOME! No matter your trauma, it does not define you. Never forget that! I've been in similar shoes. It will get better. It will be ok.

Yours,
A Fellow Survivor

Through the years of hardship and tragedy has happened to us all. If you can keep faith and look for the good, it will help strengthen you.

We will grieve, cry, ask why, and at times even blame yourselves. This is fine it's healing, but do not dwell on the negative, take small steps, lean and depend on family and friends. It will take time but your experience may help someone else, then you'll know the answers to;

Why Did this Happen to Me!!!

Through the years hardship and tragedy has happened to us all. If you can keep faith and look for the good, it will help strength you.

We will grieve, cry, ask why, and at times even blame your-selves. This is fine it's healing, but do not dwell on the negative, take small steps, lean and depend on family and friends. It will take time but your experience may help someone else, then you'll know the answer to:

Why Did this Happen to Me!!

Dear Fellow Earthling,

This place is vast and growing. I know that's hard to handle sometimes but gratitude helps, also snacks. We're on a giant blue ball hurtling around a flaming gas orb. So, like... if you think about it, the fact that you're alive and reading this is it's own miracle. Think about it; how many things don't exist right now. But you do. And that's pretty cool. Thanks for existing and stuff.
A strange friend.

Dear Fellow Earthling,

This place is vast and growing. I know that's hard to handle sometimes But gratitude helps, also snacks. We're on a giant blue ball hurtling around a flaming gas orb. So, like... if you think about it, the fact that you're alive and reading this is its own miracle. Think about it; how many things don't exist right now. But you do. And that's pretty cool. Thanks for existing and stuff.

— A strange friend

I want YOU to know that I am - like YOU - a fallible, flawed (sometimes failing, sometimes falling) human being who has been to some dark places. But, I have learned to believe in the LIGHT.

The LIGHT is waiting for YOU and belongs to YOU

I want YOU to know that I am- like YOU_ a fallible, flawed (sometimes failing, sometimes falling) human being who has been to some dark places. But, I have learned to believe in the LIGHT.

The LIGHT is waiting for YOU and belongs to YOU.

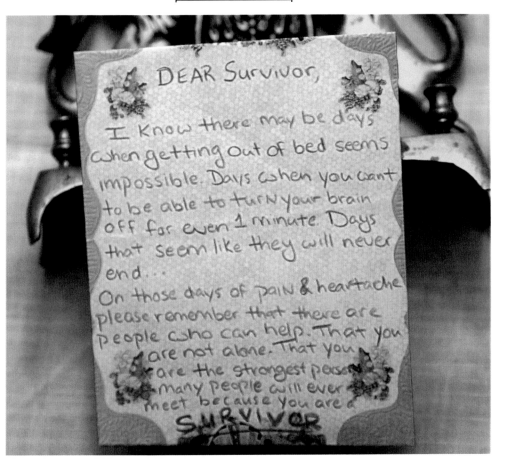

DEAR Survivor,

I know there may be days when getting out of bed seems
impossible. Days when you want to be able to turn your brain off
for even 1 minute. Days that seem like they will never end...
On those days of pain & heartache please remember that there
are people who can help. That you are not alone. That you are
the strongest person many people will ever meet becase you are
a SURVIVOR.

I am a police officer, and I want you to know that we hold special sentiment for those who've suffered at the hands of others. We care about you and want you to be strong. Recognize there is dignity and godliness in suffering. We all suffer in one way or another you will be strong

Again and you will be loved. First, love yourself.

John

I am a police officer, and I want you to know that we hold special sentiment for those who've suffered at the hands of others. We care about you and want you to be strong. Recognize there is dignity and godliness in suffering. We all suffer in one way or another. You will be strong again and you will be loved. First, love yourself.

John

Hello ~

A pet has helped me through life's ups and downs. But so have friends I called. I'd also talk to a person on the bus or in a store. Often I'd learn that they too were struggling with a life's challenge. May you share and find comfort from another. We are here for one another— you are not alone. A HUG TO YOU!

Love- from another!

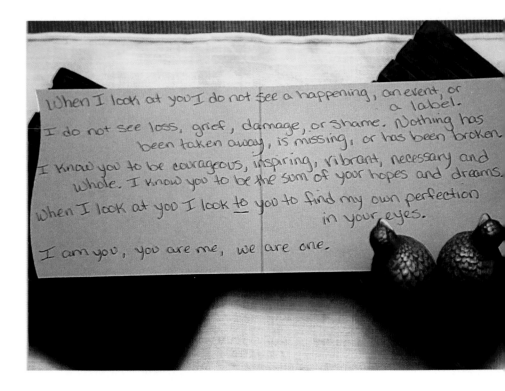

When I look at you I do not see a happening, an event, or a label.

I do not see loss, grief, damage, or shame. Nothing has been taken away, is missing, or has been broken.

I know you to be courageous, inspiring, vibrant, necessary and whole. I know you to be the sum of your hopes and dreams.
When I look at you I look to you to find my own perfection in your eyes.
I am you, you are me, we are one.

Dear Exceptional Survivor-

You fight with the light of 1000 stars- and the love of 1000 hearts!

Dear whoever is Reading This,

I am a culmination of self love and self hate. Finding the strength to conquer self hate is extremely difficult. Please do not give up. Please find beauty in the little things. Love is like an aloe plant. Every drop of water helps it grow, and once it grows it has healing properties. Aloe can grow in the desert, one of the harshest environments for a plant to grow. Yet, it grows. So can you. Never give up. Growth takes time.

With Love,
A fellow aloe plant.

Dear Whoever is Reading This,

I am a culmination of self love and self hate. Finding the strength to ~~conquer~~ conquer self hate is extremely difficult. Please do not give up. Please find beauty in the little things. Love is like a aloe plant. Every drop of water helps it grow, and once it grows it has healing properties. Aloe can grow in the desert, one of the harshest ~~conditions~~ envirnments for a plant to grow. Yet, it grows. So can you. Never give up. Growth takes time.

With Love,
A fellow aloe plant.

Dear Beautiful
People of the World:

I feel you deeply.

I acknowledge your
pain.

I am sorry.

I will ♥ be your ally.
In this together

IT'S NOT YOUR FAULT.

IT'S NOT YOUR FAULT.

IT'S NOT YOUR FAULT.

DON'T
APOLOGIZE.

IT'S NOT YOUR FAULT.

Write a reflection, reaction, or letter...

_____

_____

_____

_____

_____

_____

_____

_____

_____

_____

_____

_____

_____

_____

Feel free to send these reflections, reactions, or letters to
A Letter for You, P.O.B 472, Garrett Park, MD 20896

Bullying

I walked into a middle school classroom equipped with blank cards and curious to see what kind of letters 7th graders would produce. As a class, we crafted a definition of survivors, read the official definition from the dictionary and then the students very generously volunteered the types of things they were enduring in their own lives. I asked these students to trust me, to put their heads down and then raise their hand if I call out something they, or someone they knew had been through in the last few months. When I completed gathering data points for the list we created, I had them all pick their heads back up and I read the statistics we gathered out loud. I asked them to look around to each of their classmates. I then asked them if they knew that so many of them were struggling with their own lives, had sick family members, divorce, or different forms of trauma. They did not know who exactly was dealing with what but they were stunned by the numbers and the types of things their peers were enduring.

Bullying came up and a young man's hand shot up. He stood up for himself and said he hated being teased for being the shortest person in his grade and he shared how he felt about it. In that moment, he was the biggest and bravest person in the room. His friends looked at him differently for the first time because he drew boundaries and shared his vulnerability. I saw that his courage gained him respect and at the very least, he stood taller for having just been brave enough to speak his truth. That young man's grit was remarkable and he raised his own chin a few inches. He walked out of that room with the courage of someone not afraid of who they are. The letters the students produced have me convinced that youth is not wasted on the young; they simply need the opportunity to do good and be selfless, and they will surprise us all.

Disclaimer
If this topic is triggering, please skip this section and go to page 62

A letter for you.....

You light up the world and yet you don't see it. But I do. I always have. You matter! Don't you see? You just have to believe. You weren't a mistake so don't ever think that. Don't let these obstacles bring you down. We get through. We build. We grow. We conquer. We strive. We win. This too shall pass.

A letter for you . . . .
You light up the world and yet you don't see it. But I do. I always have. You matter! Don't you see? You just have to believe. You weren't a mistake so don't ever think that. Don't let these obstacles bring you down. We get through. We build. We grow. We conquer. We strive. We win. This too shall pass.
XO

Being Bullied is really hard. It can be so hard not to see yourself the way the bully sees you. You start taking their hate into your mind. But the ugly thoughts that are in their mind don't have to come into yours. Use some "self talk" to tell yourself it's really not about you, it's about the bully who has a sick need to hurt other people. Ignore what you can - find good people who can be in your life and help you. You Matter!

Dear Brother,
It would be a lie if I said that I knew what you are going
through, but whatever it is, you are not alone. Whether it be
bullying, or sickness, or loss, you are not alone. I know that at
the moment, it feels like you are in an endless loop of sadness, but
you are not the only one looping in sadness. If you feel like you
need to talk to someone, your friend, your family, your comrade,
don't hold back. Just remember, you are kind. You are caring. You
have a positive impact on others. You are funny.
AND YOU ARE HUMAN.

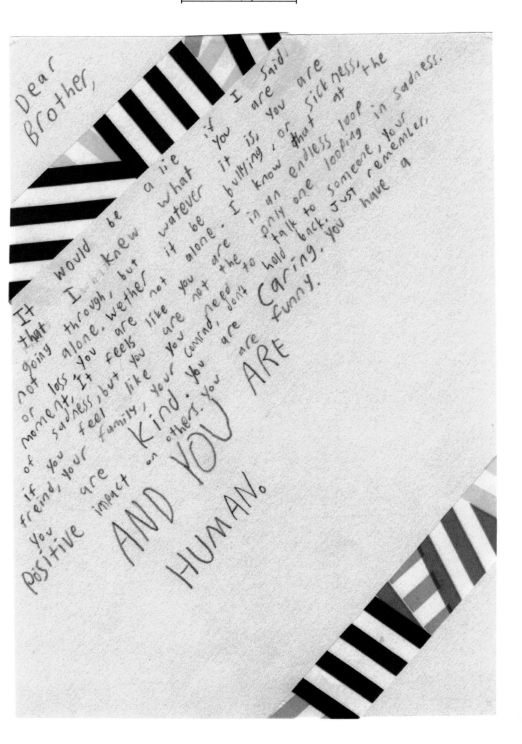

Dear Brother,

It would be a lie if I said I knew what you are going through, but whatever it is, you are not alone. Whether it be bullying, or sickness, the loss. You are not alone. I know that at the moment, It feels like you are in an endless loop in sadness, but you are not the only one looping in sadness. If you feel like you need to talk to someone, your freind, your family, your connrad, don't hold back. Just remember, you are Kind. You are Caring. You have a positive impact on others. You are funny.

AND YOU ARE HUMAN.

Being BULLIED is really hard. Sometimes it's so hard not to see yourself the way the bully sees you. You can start taking their hate into your own mind. Bullies are filled with so much anger that it spills out onto any target they pick – which might be you. Putting you down makes the bully feel better.

So try...

- to use self talk
- to ignore
- to report what's going on to someone you trust
- to know you have value
- to know you are NOT alone

Dearest friend,

    I know it is difficult to love yourself sometimes. The world tells you that other girls are more beautiful or skinny but you are more beautiful, just as beautiful as the ocean. This is hard to remember, I know that all too well, but please have confidence and be aware of your inner beauty. There is so much out in the world for you - so much hope, so much love, so much friendship, and so much faith. I truly believe in your inner and outer beauty.
    - ♡

Ever feel like you're
not fitting in?

Good.

Ever feel like you're
not fitting in?

Good.

Dear Survivor,

You are so brave! Thank you for sharing your experience. It is a lesson and an encouragement to me and for others who have been in this situation.
Thank you for your courage. God loves you and I am not afraid anymore.

Thank you.

Write a reflection, reaction, or letter...

_____

_____

_____

_____

_____

_____

_____

_____

_____

_____

_____

_____

_____

_____

_____

_____

_____

_____

Feel free to send these reflections, reactions, or letters to
A Letter for You, P.O.B 472, Garrett Park, MD 20896

Cancer

Cancer was a foreign concept to me until I met this boy in middle school. He had a gentle disposition, he was hilarious and he was kind. He was also bald and very pale, which I barely noticed until someone used the "C" word. I did not know that cancer could impact a kid. I naively assumed, like every other child, that I was immortal until I met this guy. We grew up in an area that was progressive and supportive so we were all in his corner as he healed.

He moved away at a very critical time and as an adult, he revealed to me that he'd been bullied because the kids in his new school did not understand cancer. His voice couldn't change and his hair did not grow normally due to the irreversible impact of his treatment. He looks back with such bitterness about being so misunderstood and isolated, mocked for the battle scars he gained as he fought for his very existence and right to live.

I saw him like a damn super hero. I remember telling him that as an adult, his high pitched voice and peach fuzzy hair was what his superhero and superhuman cape was made of because he didn't die. He should fly around this crazy earth with the confidence of a cat with nine lives. I wish he saw himself the way I saw him. I was saddened by the ignorance and injustice of the world. He deserved more, all of the fighters out there fighting the good fight do. The next few pages are for people struggling with illness, for their caretakers and those who are in the trenches with them.

Disclaimer
If this topic is triggering, please skip this section and go to page 70

Caring for someone you love, watching them go through this and not being able to take it away is very hard but not harder than the actual battle. Keep your head up! Keep their head up! Remember the goal and always support their dreams because in the end that's why you're their caregiver. Caregivers are the Real MVPS!

Cancer is like an invisible foe, you gotta fight that S.O.B!
With love <3

Dear Cancer Patient,

I know your journey is not easy. How? Because I am one and am undergoing a second set of twelve chemos. I want you to know that you are very important and special! Take care of yourself and hang in there. Don't give up! Smile and think positive thoughts because it does help.

A journey of a thousand miles begins with a simple step. Remember no journey is hassle free. Many obstacles come in/ become a part of the journey. So have hope and stay positive.
From Nurse

A journey of a thousand miles begins with a simple step. Remember no journey is hassle free. Many obstacles come in/ become a part of the journey. So have hope and stay positive.
From Nurse

Dear Survivor,

Be strong. Remember anything is possible through Christ who strengthens me. I pray for all cancer survivors every day. The things that helped me tremendously during treatment was family, prayer and spending time with God every day. Stay strong and persevere all things. Love you all.

Fellow
Survivor

Dear Survivor,
Be strong. Remember anything is possible through Christ who strengthens me. I pray for all cancer survivors everyday. The things that helped me tremendously during treatment was family, prayer and spending time with God every day. Stay strong and persevere all things. Love you all.
Fellow Survivor

Dear You,

Things are not easy, Buddhism says life in essence is suffering. And I think that just sucks. I lost my sister to cancer when we were 24 and I promise it gets easier - but right now - where you are in life- it's okay to feel everything and know sometime it's just HARD. You're strong. Sending you love.

Your friend.

Write a reflection, reaction, or letter...

_____

_____

_____

_____

_____

_____

_____

_____

_____

_____

_____

_____

_____

_____

_____

_____

_____

Feel free to send these reflections, reactions, or letters to
A Letter for You, P.O.B 472, Garrett Park, MD 20896

Violence

She breezed by my table on a sunny day wearing the plainest of brown dresses, though there was nothing plain about her. Wondering what the letters on the table were about, she came up to me shyly and when I invited her to write an anonymous letter for people having a hard time, she told me she could not possibly have a thing to offer anyone. I argued that anyone who can smile that warmly with a stranger must have something to offer. I handed her a pen and blank card and she knocked the wind out of my lungs when she casually mentioned that a few years ago, she was stabbed five times. I was shocked and insisted she write her wisdom down. Smiling as radiantly as she did must have taken some work and people could learn some lessons from someone so resilient.

Her smile got larger and more determined as she wrote her letter. She asked to give me a hug and I was happy to oblige. I wanted to hug this happy human who did not let the world define how she walked through her day and how she treated others. She didn't consider herself a victim, she considered herself lucky and smiled from a deep gratitude for every single day she was not promised. Survivors don't always look like they survived something. Sometimes, they gently breeze by you on a sunny day and you would never know what happened in their lives until you asked. I picked up her letter and saw that she left her personal information so that if anyone wanted to reach out to her, she would be happy to share her lessons with them. When she walked away from the table with a little skip, the human spirit surprised me again. She came to the table shy and unsure but left having contributed some of her magic to the project and having proven to me that joy is it's own victory.

Disclaimer
If this topic is triggering, please skip this section and go to page 78

To those who have laid their lives on the line for our freedoms.
I am sorry that we've made such a mess of things. Please know
that I will use my energy for peace and love and the freedom
that you fought for. Despite this blow, in my core, I believe that
Love wins.

To those who have
laid their lives on the
line for our freedom,
I'm sorry that we've
made such a mess of
things. Please know that
I will use my energy
for peace and love
and the freedom
that you fought for.
Despite this blow, in
my core, I believe that
Love wins.

Dear One who has Survived Violence,

I wish you healing and strength as you take your journey to wholeness and recovery.

May you bloom as now in Spring the trees and flowers bloom.

Sending Love...

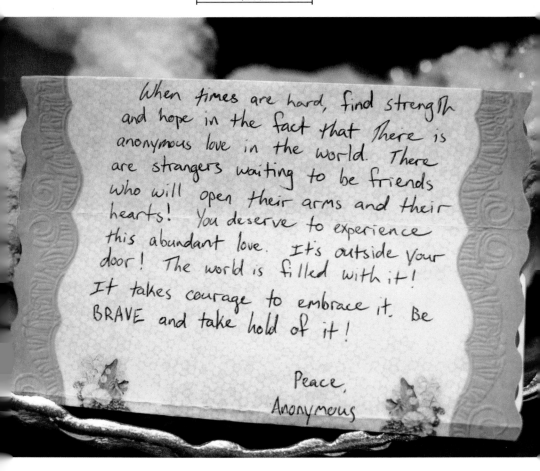

When times are hard, find strength and hope in the fact that there is anonymous love in the world. There are strangers waiting to be friends who will open their arms and their hearts! You deserve to experience this abundant love. It's outside your door! The world is filled with it! It takes courage to embrace it. Be BRAVE and take hold of it!

Peace,
Anonymous

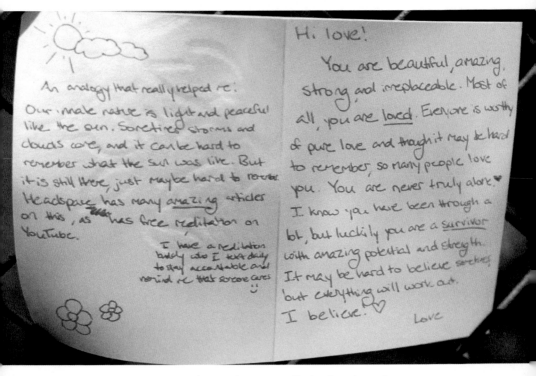

An analogy that really helped me!
Our innate nature is light and peaceful like the sun. Sometimes storms and clouds come, and it can be hard to remember what the sun was like. But it is still there, just may be hard to remember. Headspace has many amazing articles on this as has free meditation on Youtube.
I have a meditation buddy who I text daily to stay accountable and remind me that someone cares. =)

Hi love!
You are beautiful, amazing, strong and irreplaceable. Most of all, you are loved. Everyone is worthy of pure love and though it may be hard to remember, so many people love you. You are never truly alone <3 I know you have been through a lot, but luckily you are a survivor with amazing potential and strength. It may be hard to believe sometimes but everything will work out. I believe. <3
Love

I'm just a person, who honestly doesn't mean much to the world.
But I want you to know that I care.

Write a reflection, reaction, or letter...

_____

_____

_____

_____

_____

_____

_____

_____

_____

_____

_____

_____

_____

_____

Feel free to send these reflections, reactions, or letters to
A Letter for You, P.O.B 472, Garrett Park, MD 20896

LGBTQ

Two of the bravest men I knew "came-out" around the time Matthew Shepard, an involuntary martyr of the gay community, was tortured and left for dead on a fencepost simply because of his sexual orientation. I didn't know people were brutally murdered for that. They came out when it was terrifying and I was terrified for them. They loved me for no reason because they understood how it felt to be loved with conditions. I grew up, and though I was not a member of the LGBTQ community, it always welcomed me with a sense of belonging and a sense of home that was not a given for any of them. They never took love, acceptance or kindness for granted.

I found out one of my secret heroes died of complications from HIV. I did not know that people could laugh as hard as they cried during a funeral but, man, did we celebrate his life that day. My other hero died of suspected and unexpected suicide. The loss of both leaves an ache in my heart for what could have been had the world offered them the unconditional love they always so freely provided. I often wonder, if the world had been kinder, would they still be here making all of us howl with laughter today... I collect these letters to honor them and every single person who has a unique journey in love, connection and sexuality.

To LGBT Youth-

Know that your life matters. Times may be hard and you may feel alone but PLEASE know you are loved, you are valued and there is an entire community out there that will support and encourage you.

You don't have to do this alone. I love you, you & YOU.

We are here for YOU!!

The LGBT Community

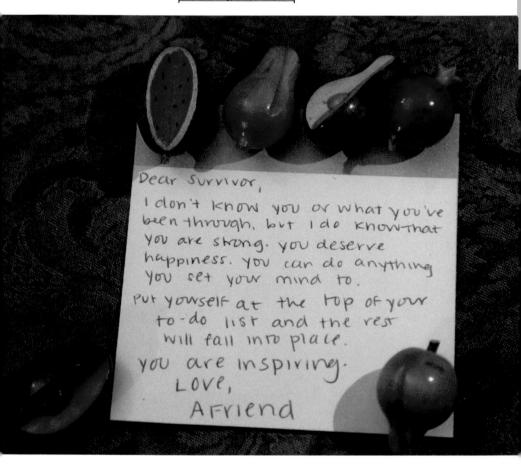

Dear Survivor,

I don't know you or what you've been through, but I do know that you are strong. You deserve happiness. You can do anything you set your mind to. Put yourself at the top of your to-do list and the rest will fall into place.
You are inspiring.

Love,
A Friend

Friend,

I understand what you are going through. Maybe not the same thing,
but I have been through heartache & hard things. I hope you find a reason
to smile today. When you smile, it makes the world a brighter place for me & you.

Love,
A friend <3

Be yourself!

If you can't count on anyone else, know that I will love you
despite your race, your sexuality,
your gender, anything.

I will always have love for your beautiful soul.

You change the world everyday just by being in it.

-Love

Love is strong
Love is kind
Love has pain
Love has hurt
Love brings joy
Love brings lessons.
Love is forever.
Love is for you.
Please love yourself &
Take joy in loves lessons.
Allow the heart to shine no matter what brings you down.

XOXOXOXOX

You ARE important, you're
Beautiful & God Loves you. Don't
take words to serious. Follow your
Dreams and always Believe in yourself
you are worth it. Being gay won't Be
so Bad, make some good friends And
love them. Trust in God and Believe
in your own self worth. your life
Belongs to you so own it. Dream,
Believe, Create, Inspire and don't
worry about love, it will find you.
trust God, trust God, trust God
no matter what. Dreams do come
true

You ARE important, you're beautiful & God Loves you. Don't take words too serious. Follow your dreams and always believe in yourself. You are worth it. Being gay won't be so bad, make some good friends and love them. Trust in God and Believe in your own self worth. Your life belongs to you so own it. Dream, Believe, Create, Inspire and don't worry about love, it will find you. Trust God, trust God, trust God, no matter what. Dreams do come true.

Write a reflection, reaction, or letter...

_____

_____

_____

_____

_____

_____

_____

_____

_____

_____

_____

_____

_____

_____

_____

_____

Feel free to send these reflections, reactions, or letters to
A Letter for You, P.O.B 472, Garrett Park, MD 20896

Sexual Assault

This project is shared with friends, families and strangers wherever I go, whenever I can. Unbeknownst to me, a friend of mine found that she was pregnant after a rape. Understandably she kept a tight lid on her situation, consulted with a doctor and scheduled an abortion. She was not ready to be a single mother and I have nothing but compassion for the difficult choices people must make in their own lives.

She somehow remembered the project I shared with her a million times over. It was one of those break-in case of emergency moments and the website was available for her when she needed it. After reading the letters, she was overwhelmed by the encouragement and inspired to brave the next chapter of her life alone. She never made it to her appointment.

The first time I held her daughter, I couldn't speak through my tears. That little girl will always be the reason I gather proof of the goodness in this world. Her mother will always inspire me to keep gathering love letters for every human being that was sexually violated and endured, regardless of their choices, how they heal and where they are in their healing process.

Disclaimer
If this topic is triggering, please skip this section and go to page 94

Dear Survivor,

    I may not know your whole Story, but your Story matters, you matter. You are strong, Stay Confident and proud of who you are. You are never alone, there are other survivors, and we stand by your Side.

Love, Someone who cares!

Dear Survivor,
I may not know your whole story, but your story matters, you matter. You are strong, stay confident and proud of who you are. You are never alone, there are other survivors, and we stand by your side.
Love,
Someone who cares!

Dear friend,

I am writing to let you know that you are not alone. Although what you are going through is unique to you, there are people out there that understand. You will make it through.

Hello,
I want you
to know I believe you. Males, the government,
ignorant people... fuck them. You are
strong. You are a hero. You have
been through the unimaginable
but you will not let this ruin
you. If you let this change
you, then your attacker wins.
I know you can get back
up. YOU ARE STRONG. ♡

Hello,
I want you to know I believe you. Males, the government,
ignorant people... fuck them. You are strong. You are a here. You
have been through the unimaginable but you will not let this ruin
you.. If you let this change you, then your attacker wins. I know
you can get back up. YOU ARE STRONG.
<3

Dear You!

As a survivor I know it's sometimes hard to believe that the "others" call you "survivor." What does that even mean you think? As you continue to live one day at a time... I wish I had better words to share, magical words to share.
Just know you are Amazing, loved and worthy.
<3

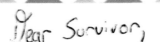

Dear Survivor,

Your body, your worth, & your sexuality, are yours, and yours alone. Never let anyone's actions or words make you believe otherwise. You are stronger than you think, and more important to me than you know. Please remember to love yourself, take life one day at a time, speak your truth. ♡

Dear Survivor,
Your body, your worth, & your sexuality, are yours, and yours alone. Never let anyone's actions or words make you believe otherwise. You are stronger than you think, and more important to me than you know. Please remember to love yourself, take life one day at a time, speak your truth. <3

To whoever gets this,
Hi. I'm a 19 year old college student. You're
going through something right now that is
an unspeakable kind of pain. I'd like you
to know, from one stranger to another,
I'm also a survivor. When I was 15 I
lost my virginity to a rapist on a
cruise. It was one of the most haunting
experiences of my life and id never wish
it upon my worst enemy. I feel for you
from the bottom of my heart. I
promise you will get through this.
you are so so strong. You're someone's
sunshine. Please don't ever
forget your worth.
All my love

To whoever gets this,
Hi. I'm a 19 year old college student. You're going through
something right now that is an unspeakable kind of pain. I'd like
you to know, from one survivor to another, I'm also a survivor.
When I was 15 I lost my virginity to a rapist on a cruise. It
was one of the most haunting experiences of my life and I'd
never wish it upon my worst enemy. I feel for you from the
bottom of my heart. I promise you will get through this. You are
so so strong. You're someone's sunshine. Please don't ever forget
your worth.
All my love

Write a reflection, reaction, or letter...

_____

_____

_____

_____

_____

_____

_____

_____

_____

_____

_____

_____

_____

_____

_____

_____

Feel free to send these reflections, reactions, or letters to
A Letter for You, P.O.B 472, Garrett Park, MD 20896

Loss / Suicide

Today my mother dances through her day and is a beam of sunshine. I love her exponentially and she is larger than life now that she has chosen to live it fully. I saw her bloom late in life. As a little girl, my mother would have mood swings that rocked my whole world. I could feel the ground shift when she was angry, but when she was sad was when fear would grip my spine and I could not find my footing. I didn't know what to do or say but I felt myself desperately try to be a "good girl" so as to not stress her out. When I saw hidden bottles in her closet, I feared opening closets and drawers because I did not know what I would find nor did I know what to do with what I actually would find.

I understood the world was in fact not fair and adults were duct-taping their lives together, too. I did not know the word for depression until I was older but I knew its sharp edges and rough terrain in my bones. Sometimes she would walk around completely listless, numb and be so far away inside. I kept thinking that I had to be the one who made her want to live. As an adult, I am not sure what was going on in my mother's head; I am not sure if she was ever going to harm herself but the fear that she might was very real for me. She took steps late in life to fall in love with herself and her life. I am grateful daily for the twinkle in her eye and the vibrations in her laughter. I do not remember the sound of it in my childhood but now she giggles often.

This section is to honor anyone feeling lost, having experienced loss or even the debilitating fear of possibly losing someone. Each angle of this experience is valid and raw and requires compassion towards yourself and others. I hope you find some of what you may need in the next few pages.

Disclaimer
If this topic is triggering, please skip this section

My friends,

Stay alive. I love you. Things will change and life can be so sweet after the bitter times. You will experience the best moments after you pull through the storm.

Dear Survivor
The world knows you're out there. We all care about you, so never
stop asking for HELP
We are all glad that you are a survivor so keep living on!

Please hang in there.
You are loved more than you know.
It will get better.
Believe that.
You will leave a hole in the heart of the universe if you go.
I can't imagine my life without my daughter.
I thank God she hung in there and didn't leave me.
Please. Don't leave.

Dear Human,

Get UP! Please... Please get up... I know you don't want to or feel like it, To tell you the truth, most days neither do I but I will make you a deal... You don't know me, I don't know you but I give you my word that I will get my ass out of bed for you everyday if you do the same for me. I will never know but I will just believe in the honor code/honor system.

I will just believe in you...

You get up and I'll get up and we will figure this all out...

Somehow....

Dear Human,
Get UP! Please... Please get up... I know you don't want to or feel like it. To tell you the truth, most days neither do I but I will make you a deal... You don't know me, I don't know you but I give you my word that I will get my ass out of bed for you everyday if you do the same for me. I will never know but I will just believe in the honor code/honor system.
I will just believe in you...
You get up and I'll get up and we will figure this all out...
Somehow...

Dear Survivor, Dear fighter, Dear hero,
Everyday that you CHOOSE is a day won. I look to you. I am
forever grateful to you, incredibly impressed by you.
An army is behind you. You are a beautiful testament to how
strong we are, how strong YOU are. You are already changing
the world. You have changed me. I am a twenty-something and
I think today my eyes were opened. Teach me, lead by example
you champion.
You are not alone.
I hope this pen finds your hand. I have you w/ a strong firm
grip of affirmation and LOVE for you. I love you. Thank you.
XX

Hi Friend,
I want you to know you are not alone. I have battled bipolar &
addiction. I thought death was my only option. We have brains
that tell us dying would be the only way out. I'm here to tell
you it's not. I was ready to leave 4 children of mine, a career,
everything, 2015 July, I came out

Hello-
If you are reading this, Its because you have suffered the devastating loss of Someone you love. I too have lived through the death of someone who I Loved very much, completing suicide. I want you to Know that you will feel joy again — it may take what seems like forever but joy will come. You will find a way to live with this hole in your heart and you will find a way to keep the legacy of your loved one's life alive! Until the Be patient with yourself. Your friend

Hello-
If you are reading this, its because you have suffered the devastating loss of someone you love. I too have lived through the death of someone who I loved very much, completing suicide. I want you to know that you will feel joy again - it may take what seems like forever but joy will come. You will find a way to live with hole in our heart and you will find a way to keep the legacy of your loved one's life alive! Until then, be patient with yourself.
Your friend

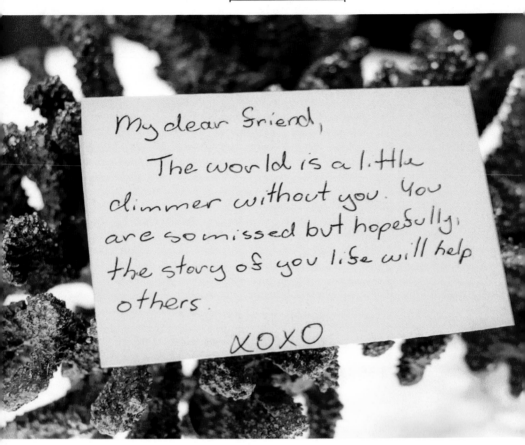

My dear friend,

The world is a little dimmer without you. You are so missed but hopefully the story of your life will help others.

XOXO

use kind words

Don't ever give up
Always Know your
Life is worth living

I lost my husband
and I have suffered
this loss over 10 yrs

Don't ever give up

Don't ever give up. Always know your life is worth living.
I lost my husband and I have suffered this loss over 10 years.
Don't ever give up.

To the beautiful person reading this, I want to tell you that I've walked the rough path as a survivor of suicide loss for 5 years now, and I'm here for you. It isn't easy and there are bad days, but keep your head up because the good days will outnumber the bad ones. Be gentle with yourself and don't be afraid to ask for help. All my love.

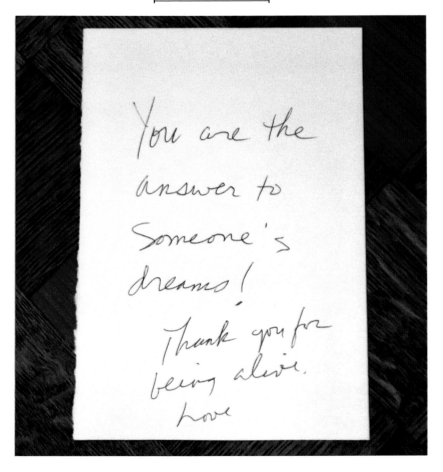

You are the answer to someone's dreams!
Thank you for being alive.

Love

For the moments you went through I am sorry. For the scars you have made, you will mend them. And for those times when you want to run away or die you will get through it. Because there are people who will listen. You may not think so, and this might not seem like a lot but I care and give a damn of what happens to you. And there are other people too. Those moments made you strong, made you who you are. Never lose that and never lose you.
But there will be sunshine for the rain.
-Stranger who cares.

For the moments you
went thourgh I am Sorry.
For the Scars you have
made, you will mend then
And for those times
when want to run away or
. die you will get thourgh it.
Because there are people,
people who will listen. you
May not think So, And this
might not seem like a lot, But
I care and give a dam
of what happens to you.
And there are other
people two. Those moment
made you Strong, made
you who you are. Never
lose that. And
Stranger   herer lose you.
who
cares,

doN't lEt tHe
SuNsHine
spOil
yOuR rAin
But there will
be sunshine
for the rain.

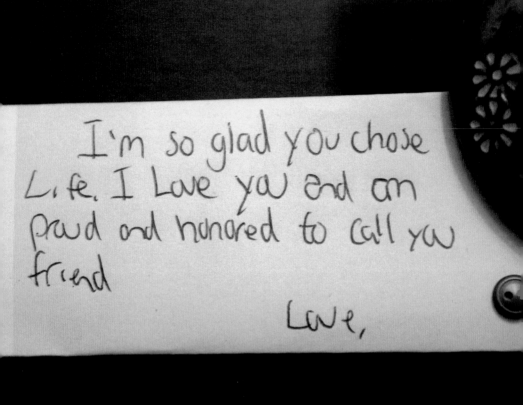

I'm so glad you chose life. I love you and am proud and honored to call you friend.

Love

Hey you awesome person!

I know right now may seem like it's an impossible time to get through. But I want you to know that you are more than capable of making it through this. I am praying for you and hoping that you don't give up even at your lowest times. I'd like for you to remember that when life says give up, HOPE whispers "try it one more time!"
I believe in you!
-xoxo <3

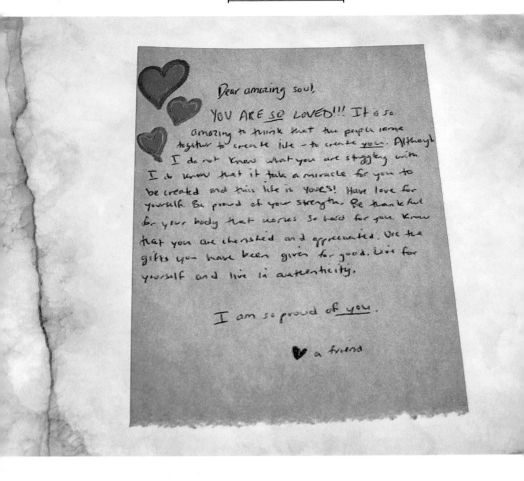

Dear amazing soul,

YOU ARE SO LOVED!!! It is so amazing to think that the people came together to create life- to create you. Although I do not know what you are struggling with I do know that it took a miracle for you to be created and this life is yours! Have love for yourself. Be proud of your strength. Be thankful for your body that works so hard for you. Know that you are cherished and appreciated. Use the gifts you have been given for good. Live for yourself and live in authenticity.
I am so proud of you.

<3 a friend

I'm sorry that the world can be so cold... BUT
You Matter to me

The end...
(Kind of)

The end of this book is the beginning of something powerful for our friends and family who have suffered in the wilderness of the world. I picture this book being passed around schools, college campuses, in waiting rooms and as gifts for friends enduring the way life tests them. I picture this project and book starting conversations people may not know how to have but can brave together. My prayer is that this project can create bridges for people who need to know that kindness exists, can be quantified and that people are rooting for every type of survivor out there with their whole damn heart.

What I have learned in the countless hugs with strangers and those who have honored me with their stories is that love coupled with authenticity is enough. Letters where thousands took the time, weighed their words, used the intimacy of their own handwriting as a unique stamp to contribute to compassion in the world is powerful when it is held in another's hands. This book was created so that survivors could physically hold another's best intentions.

Survivors do not need you to solve their problems or say the perfect thing. They may not feel like they are a problem to fix. In vulnerable moments, people only respond to the truth even if the truth is, "I do not know what to say but I will be here while you say it and I am in your corner however you need me to be." I learned this the hard way and offer it to you with humility and sincerity.

People may just want to know that they can exist in front of another human being and still be accepted regardless of their own struggles and personal demons. I have learned that individuals cope differently and trauma can be worn with a smile or a scowl, neither of which are personal to anyone in their lives. I have found that curiosity helps in compassion so when I am upset, I attempt to ask questions instead of making assumptions or declarations. I am still human and have to be compassionate with myself about how little I know and how often I make mistakes with people and so ask questions and love people through their difficulty in answer them.

Recognize your own humanity and limitations. When someone reveals something to you that is out of your depth, forward them to the right resources or ask them if they need support finding the right therapist or professional to empower them in their journey. You don't have to have the answer, just show up. If you don't know how to show up, ask them if they have any preferences or if what you are doing/not doing is okay. They will answer you to the best of their ability but be okay with the fact that they may not know how to answer you either. Be okay if people aren't okay yet. The road to recovery is just not linear.

We need more letters for all the different types of survivors out there. Please send your letters, reflections and reactions to:

A Letter For You
POB 472
Garrett Park, MD 20896

Gratitudes

First and foremost, I am profoundly grateful to the survivors and supporters of survivors that have written letters, read them and shared them with the world. This project grew organically because of each of you.

This book was accomplished and held up by a village of meaningful people, who deeply love others and so lovingly put up with me! For everyone else who has touched this project for any amount of time, sifted through any of the letters, helped me to write speeches, stood in the cold with me collecting letters from strangers and hugging them alongside me, thank you. I am grateful for everyone who helped expand the reach of this project so more survivors know of its existence.

Thank you! Thank you! Thank you Kim Bruce for your partnership and selflessness. I did not know how to do anything book related without you and you were in the trenches with me being so patient through all of my confusion.

To Stephanie Bailey, thank you for being there in the beginning of all of this madness, being supportive and solid even though it took a million years for me to get out of my own way. I appreciate your friendship and all the different moments we broke bread together.

To my internet guardian angels Mel Wingate-Bey, Kenneth To, Maxine Moore, Kim Bruce and Alyssa Manchester, thank you for managing the website and giving survivors access to these stunning letters. Without you, there would have been no way for them to have reached so many people. Websites and social media are not in my wheelhouse. Each of you helped with the impossible parts

Rachel L. Manchester, thank you for not only connecting me to your brilliant child Alyssa but also bridging the gap for her school and her friends to access the A Letter For You Project. This project has received some of the most humbling letters from those brilliant children. You are a Mama Bear through and through. I see your commitment to having children thrive always. It is beautiful and they all could use an advocate like you.

To James Daniel, the logo has served the world well. It has helped to make A Letter For You distinct and we are all so grateful for you. I still remember you thinking I was crazy when you heard I was going to do a TEDx Talk and I admitted that I did not even have a logo. You rolled up your sleeves and blessed the project without batting an eyelash, thank you!

To Mekrina and Alex Knoll, thank you for keeping me. Just keeping me safe, loved, caffeinated and always checking in on my head, health, home and heart. I cannot thank you for all the little big things and the big little things because I cannot count them all. The way you both love and serve the world inspires me to be better and more. I pinch myself a lot because our friendship truly feels like home and family.

To Laura Thron who has been a constant cheerleader and force behind this project. I am so grateful that you took the initiative to offer who you are and all that you could to this project. I cannot even count the letters or the students on college campuses that your presence has impacted. Move back to the East Coast! Jk!

Andrea Katz for lifelong friendship, dance parties and editing of everything from this book to my actual homework. I got your back always, from bullies to elegantly winging adulting.

Thank you Kathleen Mujemulta for your logistics, love and journey to vulnerability. Joni, thank you for your energy and your light. Thank you Mustang Sallie, for the levity of your laughter and the depth of you thoughts. Thank you Renee Moore for just showing up to always keep me sane, reflective and belly dancing! Felipe, thank you for holding me accountable for what impact I say I want to make in the world. I know I hide often but you never let me do it for too long. Thank you brother. Shane, I couldn't go far without your sass and loyalty which help on the hardest days. Stella, thanks for being 100% since before I could even read and write. Trish, thank you for pushing me to use my voice in the world and reminding me it makes a difference.

To the photographers Mariana C. Barros, Kim Bruce, Marcian Costa, Stella Fernandez, Mekrina Knoll, Kindra Tully, Michael Yuenger, Shai Zohav.

These photographs honor the writers and the readers so tenderly. Thank you for lending your perspective and heart to this project. I couldn't have imagined just how many more feelings pop out of the pages you created for people you will never meet. The photos are stunning.

Mom, you dance your way through your healing and I have learned my deep love and desire to help strangers by watching you play with street children and treating everyone you meet like family. Thank you for your support and love.

Daddy, your songs, your joy, and your gentleness have gotten me through some of the toughest moments in my life. You are why I laugh loudly.

I am grateful for the integrity of my brother Noel Igot and his wife Therese Igot, along with the depth of my sister January Donovan and her husband Ryan Donovan's mission. Thank you for the gift of Felicity, Jack, Jacinta, Pia, Ena, Dominic, Bo, Joseph, Ifa, Vivi, and Rock. They keep me hungry to make the world a better place because the world has just been so much better with them in it....

About Cyd Igot

Cyd Igot, founder of aletterforyou.org, has dedicated herself to the healing and empowerment of all people. Cyd has worked in the mental health field with people processing trauma, rape, abuse and violence. Her work has also included disaster relief, fundraising, logistics, delivery of food, clothing, construction materials and medicine in the Philippines in the aftermath of Typhoon Haiyan. She enjoys traveling to different parts of the world to spend time at orphanages making children laugh, teaching and making a difference where she can. In 2016, she was invited to do a TEDx Talk and asked the question, "What is a problem worthy of your life?" When Cyd was once asked this question herself, she discovered that alleviating suffering is truly a problem worthy of her life and uses the A Letter For You Project to do so.

In the course of her life, exposure to different forms of trauma and the resilience of survivors revealed to her the destructive nature of isolation, silence and shame. Her project aletterforyou.org was born from a commitment that survivors of violence, rape, trauma of all forms and bullying feel supported, safe and loved. To date, A Letter For You has collected over 3,000 handwritten letters from a wide-range of people. Her commitment to this project is to create anonymous support for survivors such that healing, empowerment and community is available to them. This project is an opportunity for survivors and their supporters to end silence and isolation. When she is not teaching or life coaching, Cyd collects letters for survivors and gathers evidence that there is good in the world.

Made in the USA
Middletown, DE
21 February 2020

84798983R10069